# Venus and Serena Williams

**Hal Marcovitz**

Mason Crest Publishers

Produced by OTTN Publishing in association with
21st Century Publishing and Communications, Inc.

MASON CREST PUBLISHERS INC.
370 Reed Road
Broomall, Pennsylvania 19008
(866) MCP-BOOK (toll free)
www.masoncrest.com

Printed in the United States of America.

First Printing

9 8 7 6 5 4 3 2 1

Library of Congress Cataloging-in-Publication Data

Marcovitz, Hal.
   Venus and Serena Williams / Hal Marcovitz.—1st printing.
      p. cm. — (Modern role models)
   Includes bibliographical references.
ISBN 978-1-4222-0494-8 (hardcover) — ISBN 978-1-4222-0781-9 (pbk.)
   1. Williams, Venus, 1980–    —Juvenile literature. 2. Williams, Serena, 1981–    —
Juvenile literature. 3. Tennis players—United States—Biography—Juvenile literature.
4. African American women tennis players—Biography—Juvenile literature.  I. Title.
GV994.A1M36 2009
796.3420922—dc22
[B]                                                            2008025067

Publisher's note:
All quotations in this book come from original sources, and contain the spelling and grammatical inconsistencies of the original text.

## CROSS-CURRENTS

In the ebb and flow of the currents of life we are each influenced by many people, places, and events that we directly experience or have learned about. Throughout the chapters of this book you will come across **CROSS-CURRENTS** reference boxes. These boxes direct you to a **CROSS-CURRENTS** section in the back of the book that contains fascinating and informative sidebars and related pictures. Go on. ▸▸

# CONTENTS

Venus (left) and Serena Williams of the United States pose with their Olympic gold medals after winning the women's doubles final match on September 28, 2000, at the Sydney Games. The two sisters took the championship title by defeating Kristie Boogert and Miriam Oremans of the Netherlands.

# 1

# Olympic Gold

**AS VENUS AND SERENA WILLIAMS PREPARED FOR** the 2000 **Olympic Games** in Sydney, Australia, there seemed to be little doubt about the outcome in the women's tennis competitions. The two sisters had been burning up the courts for months. They were arriving in Sydney at the top of their games.

Earlier that year, the sisters easily made the U.S. Olympic women's tennis team as doubles partners. Venus was also entered in the singles competition. Their selections for the squad came after Venus won two of professional tennis's top **tournaments**—Wimbledon in Great Britain and the U.S. Open in Flushing Meadows, a neighborhood in New York City. Serena also scored some impressive wins that year in Los Angeles and Hanover, Germany.

The wins were quite a turnaround for the Williams sisters. As 2000 commenced, it didn't appear that either would be very competitive. In 1999, Serena had suffered a knee injury that kept her off the court for several weeks. Later that same year, Venus suffered an injury as well. She developed tendonitis in both wrists. Tendonitis is a painful inflammation of the tendon—the tissue that connects the muscle to the bone—caused by overuse. Evidently, Venus had been training too hard. She said:

> **"**I couldn't type, I couldn't sew, I couldn't drive at one point. I couldn't hit a **backhand**. Every time I would try to hit a serve, my whole forearm would just spasm up. I was out of order.**"**

In fact, Venus's tendonitis was so bad that her father and coach, Richard Williams, suggested that his 19-year-old daughter retire from competitive tennis. He said that she had been playing for a long time and needed to take a break.

## ☀ TAUNTS FROM McENROE ☀

Venus rejected her father's advice about retiring, but she did know that she needed some rest. After five months off from professional tennis, Venus recovered and started playing again. She won at Wimbledon and the U.S. Open, then joined her sister in the Olympic competition. The sisters arrived in Sydney in September 2000 as the clear favorites to take the **gold medal** in doubles, while Venus seemed unstoppable in singles competition.

They also arrived in Australia fresh off a bit of controversy. A few weeks before the Olympics, former American tennis champ John McEnroe told a magazine that he thought the Williams sisters were overrated. McEnroe, who had dominated men's singles tennis in the 1980s, was known as much for his sharp tongue as his skill on the court. McEnroe would often throw temper tantrums during a match, arguing with referees if he disagreed with their calls. After his retirement, he continued to be a vocal observer of international tennis, and was often sought out by **journalists** for his opinions on the game.

When asked to comment on the Williams sisters, McEnroe was quick to show his disdain. "Any good college male player could beat the Williams sisters, and so could any man on the Senior Tour," he huffed. Venus responded by shrugging off the taunt. She told a reporter that she didn't have time to test McEnroe's theory but felt that if she would ever find herself in a match against a male opponent, she liked her chances of winning. She said:

As doubles partners, Serena (left) and Venus are formidable. In this March 6, 1999, photograph from a doubles match against Katrina Adams and Debbie Graham at the Evert Cup in Indian Wells, California, the Williams sisters owned the match—which they won by a score of 6-1, 6-1.

❝If you're playing a college player, they just aren't as smart. They don't understand what it is to be [tied] in a big situation. They don't understand these things. I played a lot of guys that were stronger than me, and I was smarter.❞

## ⟫ WINNING THEIR MEDALS ⟪

Once in Sydney, the Williams's dispute with McEnroe was soon forgotten as the sisters got down to the business of beating all challengers. Venus easily steamrolled through the women's singles

**Serena stays ready as Venus leaps to smash the ball during the women's doubles final game of the 2000 Summer Olympics, held in Sydney, Australia. Sidelined for several months by injuries before the Olympics, Venus got back in shape in time to win two gold medals—for the women's singles and women's doubles tennis events.**

competition. On September 20, she faced Russian Elena Dementieva in the finals.

Major tournament matches typically take two hours or more: the players must win a majority of the games in two out of three six-game sets. In her match against Dementieva, Venus dispatched the Russian in two sets, taking a mere 58 minutes.

The next day, Venus teamed with her sister to face Dutch players Miriam Oremans and Kristie Boogert for the gold medal in the doubles competition. Again, the sisters were dominating, hitting **volleys** that overwhelmed Oremans and Boogert. Just 50 minutes after the match commenced, Venus prepared to serve for **match point**. Serena told her sister to serve an ace; it would be the perfect way to end the match. In tennis, an ace is a serve that the opponent fails to return.

## CROSS-CURRENTS

To learn about another American athlete who starred at the 2000 Olympic Games, read "The Tragedy of Marion Jones." Go to page 49. ▶▶

An instant later, Venus rocketed the ball toward Boogert. The player, although overpowered by the shot, somehow managed to get her racket on the ball. Boogert's shot lifted the ball into a high lob. As the ball descended across the net, Serena moved beneath it. Before the ball could bounce, Serena slammed it hard. It whisked by the Dutch players in a yellow blur. Match over. The Williams sisters had won the gold medal.

Moments later, Venus and Serena took their places on the medals stand. Each sister was presented with a bouquet of roses. As the medals were placed around their necks, the American flag was raised over their heads while the public address speakers played the *Star-Spangled Banner*. Both sisters said they were touched by the experience. Serena told a reporter from the *Boston Globe*:

> **❝**We worked so hard for this. The anthem, the roses, the medals . . . I'd seen it on TV. But to happen to us . . . you want to hold on to that. It might never happen again.**❞**

During a tennis lesson with her coach and father, Richard Williams, a young Venus discusses the best place her racket should contact the ball. Hours of practice on the asphalt courts of Compton, Los Angeles, soon helped Richard's youngest daughters, Venus and Serena, develop into world-class professional tennis players.

# 2

# Moments of Triumph and Bitterness

**COMPTON, CALIFORNIA, IS HARDLY THE TYPE OF** place where one would expect to find future world-class tennis players. For many years, tennis has been a sport played at its highest levels in expensive private clubs. Compton, on the other hand, is the fourth most dangerous city in the United States, known for its high murder rate and gang warfare.

But Compton, a **suburb** of Los Angeles, is where Venus and Serena Williams grew up and learned to play tennis. They did not get their education in the game on lush grass courts manicured by professional landscapers, but rather in urban playgrounds, where their feet and knees took a pounding on the hard, **asphalt** surfaces. When Richard Williams took his girls to a playground for practice, he would first have to sweep broken glass and discarded **crack cocaine** vials off the court. Occasionally, when the girls practiced, they would hear gunshots in the neighborhood.

Richard and Oracene (Brandi) Williams moved to Compton after their daughters were born. Venus was born on June 17, 1980, in nearby Lynwood, California. Serena was born September 26, 1981, in Saginaw, Michigan, where the family lived briefly. Venus and Serena joined three older half sisters in the family, Yetunde, Isha, and Lyndrea Price, Brandi's daughters from an earlier marriage.

**Serena (left) and Venus pose with their mother, Oracene, in a 1999 photograph. That year the two sisters would face each other for the first time in a championship game final. "It's a win-win situation," Venus has said of her mother's predicament when the two sisters compete against each other. "One daughter is going to win. What's the difference?"**

Richard Williams believed that big-time athletics would be his daughters' ticket out of Compton. One Sunday afternoon, Williams found himself watching a women's tennis match on TV. The tournament winner was awarded a $75,000 prize. It was in that moment that Williams decided to teach his girls how to play tennis.

He taught all five girls the game, but Venus and Serena seemed to pick up the sport much faster than their older sisters. And since they were the youngest, Williams believed they had the most potential. Soon, he concentrated his efforts on honing his youngest daughters' talents.

## ⟫ TURNING PRO ⟪

By the time the girls were in their early teens, they were already the talk of Southern California tennis circles. In fact, Serena won her first tournament before she was five years old, and by the time she was 10, she had already won 49 tournaments. Venus had compiled an equally impressive record as well, earning the rank of top tennis player under the age of 12 in Southern California.

In 1991, when Venus was 11 and Serena 10, Richard Williams decided that he had taken his daughters as far as he could and that what they needed now was professional coaching. That year, he moved the family to Florida so that his daughters could train at a tennis academy headed by Rick Macci, a nationally renowned coach who had turned several young players into world-class stars. Bob Ryland, one of the coaches who worked with Venus and Serena at Macci's school, recalled:

> **You could see they were going to be special players even then. You could see their personalities, too. Venus was always the very polite young lady . . . Serena, she was mean: 'I don't wanna do that anymore. I wanna do what Venus is doing.' When Serena was ready to stop practicing, she'd just walk off that court. That's it.**

Both girls turned professional at the age of 14. By then, they had developed the individual styles that would enable them to dominate their opponents. Venus could call on her strength and height—she would grow to 6 feet 1 inch (185.4 centimeters)—to slam shots with incredible power. Equally strong but four inches shorter, Serena developed quickness to compensate for an injury suffered at the age of 15. Playing hooky from school to ride her new skateboard, Serena fell and bruised her left wrist. As a right-handed player, she used her left hand to support her backhand stroke; but the injury made her wince every time she had to return a backhand shot. She adapted by becoming quicker on the court so that she could position herself to mostly use her **forehand** stroke.

## ⇒ REACHING THE FINALS ⇐

As young teens, both girls made quiet climbs through the rankings. They were held back, to a degree, by their father, who limited them to a handful of tournaments a year to keep them from missing too much school. Still, behind the scenes, tennis insiders were watching the sisters with quiet awe, knowing that in a brief time both would become major players on the international tour. For Venus, that moment arrived in 1997 when she played her way into the finals of the U.S. Open, one of the four tennis tournaments that make up the "Grand Slam." The other Grand Slam events are Wimbledon, the French Open in Paris, and the Australian Open in Melbourne.

**CROSS-CURRENTS**

To find out more about the four most important pro tennis tournaments held each year, read "The Grand Slam." Go to page 50. ▶▶

Prior to the 1997 tournament, Venus was ranked 66th in the world, so she would be entering unseeded. (In women's tennis, rankings are awarded by the sport's governing body, the Women's Tennis Association. Each player is awarded points for success in tournament play.)

"Seeded" means that as one of the highest-ranking players in the sport, the competitor will be matched throughout the tournament against less talented players to help ensure that the finals feature the two best players in the competition. As an unseeded player, Venus had to battle her way through a series of better-known rivals until she finally reached the finals, where she faced another teenager, Martina Hingis, the top-ranked female player in the world.

**CROSS-CURRENTS**

To learn about an incident that occurred between Venus and Irina Spirlea in 1997, read "The Bump." Go to page 51. ▶▶

Hingis quickly disposed of Venus, taking just over an hour to beat her in two **straight sets**. Venus started off strong but then committed a series of errors, hitting the ball wildly and with

In 1999, the year Venus Williams turned 19 years old, she had already established herself as a strong contender in women's tennis. In 1997 the six-foot, one-inch athlete had become the first unseeded woman ever to reach the U.S. Open final. The following year, she had won her first championship title at the IGA Tennis Classic.

too much power, sending it streaking across the back line. After the match, Venus said:

> **❝I guess I was nervous. It's natural to be nervous in a situation like that. Playing against Martina is a different match. You can't always hit your way out of it . . . I think that maybe I just thought I had to do too much.❞**

## ➤ THE DAY BELONGED TO SERENA ➤

Meanwhile, 1997 was also a big year for Serena. That year, she broke into the ranking of the top 100 players in the world when she defeated former star Monica Seles in a match in Chicago. A year later, she teamed with Belarusian tennis player Max Mirnyi to win the **mixed doubles** at Wimbledon. By 1999, Serena was ranked among the top 20 female players in the world.

That September, Serena found herself facing Hingis in the finals of the U.S. Open. Venus had entered the tournament as well but lost to Hingis in a grueling three-set semifinal match. A day later, she sat in the grandstands, watching her little sister play for a Grand Slam title.

Serena used her power and speed effectively during the match. She also kept her composure, making fewer mistakes against Hingis than Venus had committed two years earlier. Hingis played a hard game, but the day belonged to Serena. She defeated Hingis in straight sets to win her first Grand Slam title. After the match, she told reporters:

> **❝I was thinking, 'Should I scream? Should I yell? Should I cry? What should I do?' I guess I ended up doing them all.❞**

As for Venus, observers couldn't help but notice that she did not seem enthusiastic about her sister's triumph at the U.S. Open. During the match, TV cameras caught her sulking in her seat with a sour look on her face. Later, Venus admitted that her bitterness stemmed not from the jealousy of watching Serena win the Grand Slam title, but from the realization that she still had some work to do if she truly wanted to join the tennis elite. Sitting in the grand-

**Shorter and younger than her sister, 17-year-old Serena Williams was the first of the two to win a Grand Slam title. On September 11, 1999, she defeated the number one player in the world, Martina Hingis, 6-3, 7-6, to claim the U.S Open championship title. In this photo, Serena holds the winner's trophy in triumph before a cheering crowd in Flushing Meadows, New York.**

stand at Flushing Meadows, Venus resolved to improve her game. She said:

> **"I just took on a new attitude: I'm going to go for it. I'm going to get the job done. I'm not going to hold back."**

Venus (right) talks with her opponent and sister Serena before their March 28, 1999, match at the Lipton Tennis Championships, in Key Biscayne, Florida. Venus defended her title with a 6-1, 4-6, 6-4 victory over Serena in the first ever sisters final. The following October Serena would avenge her defeat by beating Venus to win the Compaq Grand Slam Cup in Munich.

# Sister Against Sister

**FOLLOWING THE U.S. OPEN, VENUS DEDICATED** herself to training. Correcting her mistakes would eventually pay off on the court, but not right away. She pushed herself too hard and developed tendonitis in both wrists, an inflammation of the tendons responsible for joint movement. The injury is common in tennis players. It kept Venus out of competition for several months.

After resting her sore wrists, Venus prepared for another Grand Slam competition: Wimbledon. But she wasn't going alone. Serena was entering the singles competition as well.

## ⇒ RIVALRY AT WIMBLEDON ⇐

Serena did well at the 2000 Wimbledon championships but lost in a semifinal match—to Venus. Over the years, as the two sisters climbed in the rankings, it was inevitable that they would face one another in major competitions. At the beginning of their careers, their father had occasionally withdrawn one of them from a tournament if it appeared that they would have to play each other. Richard Williams was not sure they could handle the emotional burden of trying to beat one another in major competitions. He said:

> **"I never would allow that when they were little kids, because it would tarnish the family. To be honest, I didn't want them to play one another head to head on the . . . tour either."**

As the sisters grew older, though, Williams let them chart the courses for their own careers and, as he had expected, the sisters faced each other from time to time. But the 2000 Wimbledon match marked the first time they had ever squared off in a Grand Slam event. Venus and Serena went against each other with a fierce resolve, rocketing serves at each other and firing them back with equally powerful shots.

**CROSS-CURRENTS**

Read "Wimbledon" to learn more about one of the most prestigious tennis tournaments held each year. Go to page 51. ▶▶

In time, Venus wore Serena down, causing her to make mistakes. In the final game, with the match on the line, Serena double faulted, meaning she failed to hit a successful serve over the net in two tries. That mistake cost her the point, the game, the set, and the match.

After the match, Richard Williams made his way down from the grandstand to courtside, where he congratulated his older daughter and consoled his younger one. He said:

> **"She takes losing harder than Venus. It's almost like dying for her. I congratulated Serena. They both played good. But I had to get her on the phone to her mama in Florida before she started to come out of it."**

After the win against her sister, Venus advanced to the final, where she faced defending Wimbledon champion Lindsay Davenport. Venus defeated her in straight sets to take the championship. After the match, Venus accepted the Wimbledon trophy from England's duchess of Kent. She told the crowd:

This picture captures the moment just before Venus (left) and Serena begin their women's singles semifinal match at the Wimbledon 2000 tennis tournament. The match between the two sisters, which took place on July 6, 2000, saw Venus defeat her sister, 6-2, 7-6. Venus would go on to win the final match and earn her first Grand Slam trophy.

**"**It's really great because I've worked so hard all my life to be here. It's strange. I always dream I win a Grand Slam. When I wake up, it's a nightmare. Now that I've got it, I don't have to wake up like that any more.**"**

**Venus Williams holds up her trophy after defeating Lindsay Davenport in straight sets, 7-6, 6-4, to win the Pilot Pen tennis tournament in New Haven, Connecticut, on August 25, 2001. Her consistent string of tournament wins ensured that Venus reached number one in the WTA rankings in February 2002.**

A few months later, Venus faced Davenport again in the finals of another Grand Slam event—the U.S. Open. Serena sat in the stands, watching her sister play. Venus dominated Davenport a second time in straight sets.

## ⟫ BEST FRIENDS ⟪

Venus and Serena's rivalry on the court continued, and so did their success. Venus won a string of tournaments in 2001, including titles again at Wimbledon and the U.S. Open. By the beginning of 2002, Venus was ranked number one in the world.

**CROSS-CURRENTS**

To learn about two great African-American players who helped open the way for the Williams sisters, read "Trailblazers." Go to page 52. ▶▶

Serena put the experience of Wimbledon behind her and racked up her own string of tournament wins. In May 2002, the sisters faced each other again in the finals of another Grand Slam tournament: the French Open. This time, Serena won. In fact, she beat her sister in Grand Slam finals twice more that year—at Wimbledon and at the U.S. Open. Thanks to those wins, Serena replaced Venus as the top-ranked player in the world—a distinction she would hold for 57 consecutive weeks.

In an interview, Serena spoke about the on-court rivalry with her older sister:

> **❝It's never been easy for me to play Venus. Beating her was a bit of a mental block for me. To finally win a match against Venus in a big tournament was a pretty big confidence booster. I learned that it's OK to do well against your sister.❞**

## ⟫ THE DARK SIDE OF CELEBRITY ⟪

As their rivalry continued throughout 2002, the sisters found themselves on the covers of magazines as well as the front pages of newspaper sports sections. Their matches were televised to audiences that totaled in the millions. Clearly, Venus and Serena were now international celebrities. But the sisters would soon learn that there can be a dark side to celebrity status.

As Serena played in Wimbledon in 2002, British police arrested a man who had been stalking her—following her from tournament to tournament in Germany, Italy, Britain, France, and the United States. He was identified by police as Albert Stromeyer, a 34-year-old German man.

Professional tennis players are particularly wary about stalkers. In 1993, Monica Seles had been the top-ranked female player in the world. As she played in a match, a man suddenly emerged from the grandstands and assaulted her with a knife, stabbing her in the back. Seles recovered from the wound but spent two years away from tennis as she dealt with the mental **trauma** of the attack. Although Seles eventually returned to competition, she was never the same player she had been before the attack.

The authorities did not want to see Serena suffer the same fate. Once, Stromeyer had shown up at a hotel in Arizona where Serena was staying during a tournament. When he demanded to see her, he was briefly detained by police. Later, a similar incident occurred in Italy. Prior to Wimbledon, police in Arizona and Italy contacted the British police and warned them to be on the lookout for Stromeyer. When they saw him approach the gates to the All England Club, they quickly moved in to detain him.

When he was arrested, Stromeyer admitted that he had been stalking Serena but insisted he meant her no harm. British prosecutor Martin Fox said Stromeyer told police that he loved her and would never hurt her. Stromeyer was charged with the minor offense of "breaching the peace." He paid a small fine and was released.

After the incidents in Arizona and Italy, Serena had started traveling with a **bodyguard**. When told of Stromeyer's arrest at Wimbledon, she shrugged off the danger, saying:

> **"**I don't really pay attention to anything like that. But I don't see how it could affect my game, him being arrested. I'm a strong person. I try not to let things like that affect me. **"**

Later that summer, Stromeyer turned up again—this time at Flushing Meadows, where Serena had entered the U.S. Open. He was arrested again; this time, he was sent back to Germany where he was placed in the custody of his parents and ordered to seek psychiatric care. Richard Williams reacted harshly to the news that Stromeyer had been stalking his daughter again.

❝Would [anything] stop me from killing this guy if he did something to one of my daughters? I don't think all the police officers in the world could stop me.❞

## ➤ DOMINATING THE SPORT ⬅

Despite the incidents with the stalker, Serena's game was as good as ever. She and Venus seemed unstoppable. The rest of the tennis

**Serena signals that she is number one after defeating Jennifer Capriati, 7-5, 7-6, during a March 30, 2002, match held at the Tennis Masters Series, in Key Biscayne, Florida. Serena's powerful performances during the WTA Tour in 2002 resulted in her taking over the number one world ranking from her sister in July of that year.**

world could do little but sit back and watch the Williams sisters rack up win after win. Asked to comment on the sisters' control of the Grand Slam finals, Lindsay Davenport said their dominance was among the most amazing feats in sports. Meanwhile, the sisters' old foe John McEnroe weighed in, complaining that when Venus played Serena, fans were shortchanged because neither sister gave it her best game.

> **It's been sloppy. It would be better if they figured out a way [to play] their best tennis against each other. I don't know if [they] need a little animosity or what.**

As for the sisters themselves, they had learned to keep their on-court rivalry apart from their off-court relationship. Indeed, away from tennis the two sisters remained best friends. Said Serena:

> **Venus is more than a great tennis player and a partner. She is a great older sister, friend, and person. Seeing that others are being helped, making sure her family is doing OK, and, above all, making sure that little sis is safe, are what truly mean the most to her.**

The Williams sisters also continued to live together. They were sharing a mansion in Florida that they had purchased with their considerable winnings. (They named the mansion *La Maison des Soeurs*—French for "house of the sisters.") By 2003, each sister's annual winnings totaled more than $12 million.

What's more, Venus and Serena each signed lucrative **endorsement** deals with shoe companies as well as sporting goods companies, sportswear manufacturers, credit card companies, and restaurant chains. Their shoe deals were particularly profitable. Venus signed an endorsement deal with Reebok, while Serena agreed to endorse Puma shoes. Each deal was valued at $40 million or more. In 2003, the Williams sisters both made *Forbes* magazine's list of the 100 wealthiest and most powerful celebrities.

Their rise in popularity meant that the two sisters were often the subject of stories speculating about their rivalry. In response, Serena has said:

**Venus (left) and Serena announce the kickoff of the "Doublemint Feel the Green" charity Internet auction on March 20, 2003. The sisters auctioned off a private tennis lesson with Serena, tennis outfits, and other items to help raise money for the Tom Joyner Foundation. The foundation provides scholarships to students at historically black colleges and universities.**

❝Tennis is just a game, and we're entertainers. People come to see us play and perform. After that, we go home, and Venus will always be my sister, we're always going to be a family. No matter what, she's always going to be there. We just take tennis as it comes. We play a match. After that, we have to be able to separate tennis from family life.❞

Many people praised the Williams sisters. Venus and Serena's success shows that African Americans can be successful in any sport, NBA star Kobe Bryant has said:

❝So many minorities think there's only basketball and football. Now they have these girls doing their thing. I stay glued to the TV when they're playing.❞

Beginning around 2003, both Venus (right) and Serena Williams began to focus on new interests outside of professional tennis. Venus turned to clothing and home design, eventually founding her own interior design company. Serena pursued an acting career. At the same time, both talented superstars continued to practice their game and participate in the WTA Tour.

# A Whole New Direction

**FOLLOWING HER THREE GRAND SLAM LOSSES TO** Serena in 2002, Venus decided to take a step back from tennis. She felt tired, and contemplated retirement. She had other interests to pursue. In fact, both sisters expressed an interest in fashion design, and Venus started taking classes in design at the Art Institute of Fort Lauderdale in Florida.

After taking the classes, Venus was ready to begin designing professionally—not only clothes, but home interiors as well. In 2003, she established her own interior design company, V Starr Interiors. Venus did not completely give up tennis that year, but she played in far fewer tournaments. She said that it was a relief taking a break from the constant press attention and questions about the rivalry with her sister. She said,

> **❝I wanted to get away from all that junk. You could be watching a men's match, a women's match or**

**CROSS-CURRENTS**

Read "Jehovah's Witnesses" to learn more about the religion to which Venus and Serena Williams adhere. Go to page 53. ▶▶

a doubles match, and all they'd talk about was the Williams sisters . . . That's just silly. "

Venus continued to play and practice to keep her skills refined, but now she found herself mixing in time on the court with meetings with clients who hired her to decorate their homes and offices. She also met regularly with contractors and took many business trips to search for art, furniture, and fabrics.

V Starr Interiors is a team effort among Venus, Denise Chernoff, Meighan Coger, and Joan Cain. The company offers a number of interior design services, from initial floor plans all the way up through paint colors and furniture placement. The portfolio on the company's Web site boasts photos of a variety of rooms, all richly decorated in many different styles. The company says that it designs for each individual client rather than promoting a signature "look." By the end of 2003, V Starr Interiors was projecting $1 million in gross sales.

The fact that Venus had committed herself so completely to her business came as no surprise to friends and family members. Of the two sisters, Venus had always been regarded as the more serious.

## ACTING CAREER

Serena, on the other hand, had always been regarded as the more fun-loving of the two sisters. As she climbed in the rankings and established herself as one of the top players in the world, Serena reveled in her celebrity status. She dyed her hair platinum blonde and cut something of a fashion figure on the court, playing in the U.S. Open in a form-fitting black Spandex catsuit. In addition, she found herself much in demand as a guest on celebrity interview shows. She made two appearances on *The Tonight Show with Jay Leno* and presented awards on ESPN's *Espy Awards*, the *MTV Music Awards*, and the *Teen Choice Awards*.

She also bought an apartment in Los Angeles and took acting lessons with an eye toward an eventual film career. On television, she has played roles in such dramatic series as *Law & Order: Special Victims Unit*, *The Division*, and *Street Time*, as well as the comedy *My Wife and Kids*. Also, she voiced characters on the animated series *Avatar: The Last Airbender*, *Higglytown Heroes*, and *Loonatics Unleashed*.

Seeded number two at the Australian Open tennis tournament in Melbourne, Venus prepares to serve against Nicole Pratt of Australia in the fourth-round match, held on January 19, 2003. Williams won 6-3, 6-2, and advanced to the quarterfinals. She would ultimately lose to her top-ranked younger sister, Serena, during the final.

**Ford**

**TIED TO THE CAUSE**

Serena Williams makes a social statement, wearing the Ford silk scarf as a symbol of solidarity in the fight against breast cancer. The 2003 Ford breast cancer awareness scarf, designed by Lily Pulitzer, is available now in-store, online and by phone from Bloomingdale's. Turn the page for details.

Serena appears in an advertisement for the 2003 Ford Motor Company's "Get Tied to the Cause" campaign. She and other celebrities were asked to wear Ford breast cancer awareness silk scarves in ads to promote sales of the scarves. The proceeds, which ultimately amounted to more than $1 million, benefited the Susan G. Komen Breast Cancer Foundation.

In 2003, Serena had to take several months off the tennis tour after undergoing knee surgery. The knee had been bothering her for years and running on it had become increasingly painful. Doctors diagnosed the problem as a partially torn tendon just below her left knee. Somehow, she had always been able to endure the pain while playing tennis but, finally, she could not ignore the injury any longer. One day, while bending down to pick up an earring, she found herself in incredible pain. She finally consented to having surgery. Although she missed playing in some important tournaments—and, as a result, lost her number one ranking to Belgian star Kim Clijsters—Serena appreciated the opportunity to explore other interests as well, particularly acting. She said:

> **"I love tennis. It's always my first love, and I really, really miss it, but in a way it is kind of a relief to see that, wow, this actually gives me a chance to do some other stuff, some acting especially."**

**CROSS-CURRENTS**

To find out about some of Venus and Serena's off-court activities, check out "Favorite Hobbies." Go to page 54. ▶▶

In fact, Serena was recuperating from knee surgery when she was asked to play a small role on *Street Time*, a series about parole officers and the former prison inmates they supervise. The series ran for two years starting in 2002 and starred veteran actor Rob Morrow (*Northern Exposure*, *Numb3rs*) as Kevin Hunter, an inmate on parole. The show followed Hunter's attempts to put his life back together now that he was out of prison, with the help of his parole officer, James Liberti, played by Scott Cohen. Originally, Serena's role—a former gang member named Meeka Hayes—was to have been minor, but when the producers learned that she did not have to keep commitments on the tour and would be able to spend more time on the set, they expanded the role and gave her a much meatier part.

## ⇒ TRAGEDY IN COMPTON ⇐

Because of their busy off-the-court careers, the Williams sisters saw a lot less of each other—and a lot less of their other family members as well. In 2002, Richard and Oracene Williams had divorced. The girls stayed close to their mother, but their father, who had always made it a point to go to all their matches, now attended only a handful a year.

As for their older half sisters, Isha had graduated from law school and was working as an attorney. Lyndrea worked as a Web page designer and part-time actress, and Yetunde worked as a registered nurse and beauty salon owner in Compton.

On the morning of September 14, 2003, the members of the Williams family received some devastating news: Yetunde Price had been killed by a gunshot that morning on a Compton street. Yetunde had been riding with her boyfriend, Rolland Wormley, in a white sport utility vehicle when their vehicle was suddenly hit by gunshots. Wormley sped away, but Yetunde had been struck in the head by one of the bullets. Wormley drove Yetunde to a hospital, but doctors were unable to save her life. Yetunde had been the mother of three young children.

Venus learned of her half sister's death while on a business trip to New York, where she had been attending the events that are part of the city's Fashion Week. Serena had been working on the *Street Time* set in Toronto, Canada, when she was told of the shooting. Both sisters hurried to Los Angeles. Raymone Bain, a spokesperson for the Williams sisters, told the media:

**❝When [Venus and Serena] received the calls from all of us here, they were saying, 'Are you sure this is correct?' They couldn't believe it. They're devastated. ❞**

Venus and Serena had been particularly close to Yetunde. For a time, their older sister had worked as their personal assistant, keeping track of their appointments, making travel arrangements, and doing other tasks that the two stars did not have time to address on their own.

## ⸎ HUNG JURIES ⸎

Police quickly made two arrests in the murder, identifying the suspects as Aaron Michael Hammer and Robert Edward Maxfield, both of whom were known to be gang members in Compton. According to police, Maxfield, armed with an assault weapon, had been waiting to ambush a white SUV that he suspected would be carrying rival gang members. Evidently, he mistook Wormley's vehicle for the gang car. Hammer was charged as well because he had been with Maxfield when the shooting occurred.

Both men were charged with murder and went on trial in 2004. In both cases, the trials ended in "hung juries"—meaning jurors could not agree unanimously on their verdicts. Typically, cases end in hung juries when prosecutors fail to produce enough evidence for guilty verdicts but jurors are not completely convinced of the defendant's innocence, either. In Hammer's case, the judge dismissed the charges, but prosecutors tried again to convict Maxfield. When the second trial was held, once again the jury could not agree on a verdict.

Finally, in 2006, Maxfield agreed to a plea bargain, meaning the prosecution dropped the most serious charge in exchange for a guilty plea and a lighter sentence. In Maxfield's case, he pleaded no contest to voluntary **manslaughter**—a lesser charge than murder—and was sentenced to 15 years in prison. Serena attended the sentencing and told the judge just how much Maxfield had hurt the Williams family. Later, Serena said:

> **"No one knows that pain, of [losing] someone you talk to every day. You still talk to their kids every day. You see how close our whole family is."**

Following Yetunde's death, Venus and Serena both had difficulty putting their tennis careers back on track. Neither sister played in many tournaments in 2004, mostly because of injuries as well as their off-the-court responsibilities. As a result, both sisters found themselves drifting down in the rankings.

## ⧫ CHARITABLE WORKS ⧫

As part of their investment into life off the tennis court, Venus and Serena devoted themselves to charitable work. In 2004, they became active in World Children's Day, which is sponsored by McDonald's restaurants. Each year on November 20, the McDonald's corporation donates sales of Big Macs and Egg McMuffins at its 30,000 restaurants to children's charities. To participate in World Children's Day, Venus and Serena organized the McDonald's Williams Sisters Tour, a series of exhibition matches that aid children's charities. During the first three years of the tour, the sisters raised more than $400,000 for programs that provide food and medical care to disadvantaged children.

Additionally, the sisters found themselves serving as role models for young urban African Americans, many of whom were unfamiliar with the sport of tennis. Arlen Kantarian, chief executive of the U.S. Tennis Association, said that Venus and Serena had become ambassadors for tennis to the black community, much as Tiger Woods had for professional golf. Their success had inspired many young blacks to learn how to play the game.

Jon Wertheim, a senior writer for *Sports Illustrated*, commented that their impact on the tennis world went beyond young blacks.

**Venus works with the staff at a McDonald's restaurant in celebration of World Children's Day. She and Serena participated in the November 20, 2003, fundraiser that took place in thousands of restaurants around the world. The event was part of a global fundraising initiative to raise money within a 24-hour period to support Ronald McDonald House Charities and other children's causes.**

Serena instructs a young girl at a March 2005 clinic held at the Ashe-Buchholz Tennis Center. Located at Moore Park, in Miami Florida, the center offers free after-school tennis and educational programs. Because Serena and Venus have been so successful in professional tennis, they have inspired many kids to learn the game.

Their youth and style, he said, attracted many young people to the sport:

> **"It's not just the [sisters'] race, it's the prestige of tennis—making it a cooler, hipper sport."**

# HOW TO PLAY
# TENNIS

Learn how to play the **Williams** sisters' way

## Venus and Serena Williams

Venus and Serena Williams had returned in full force to the courts by the time their book *How to Play Tennis* appeared in bookstores in the summer of 2004. It includes personal anecdotes, information on basic rules of the game, recommended clothing to wear and equipment to use, and much more advice for anyone who wants to learn the game.

# 5

# Returning to Form

**AFTER THEIR TIME OFF FOR VARIOUS PERSONAL** and professional reasons, it was time for the Williams sisters to get back into the game. Despite a desire to return to the court, Serena did not play competitively until mid-2003. She won just two tournaments that year, neither of them Grand Slam events.

Her injured knee still required rehabilitation, and Serena found herself consumed, as Venus had been, with opening her own business. Serena started a fashion design studio, which she named Aneres Designs. (Aneres is Serena spelled backwards.) The company defines its mission as providing clothes that make women feel beautiful and sexy. The company strives to develop a style all its own—one it calls "complex simplicity."

Venus had a similarly frustrating time. She suffered from nagging injuries to her ankles as well as an **abdominal** strain. She recovered enough to play in the Nasdaq-100 Open, but it was a poor showing. Venus went into the tournament ranked second, but she lost to the fifth-ranked player, Elena Dementieva.

In the Nasdaq-100, Venus served 11 double faults. She also racked up 51 unforced errors. Unforced errors occur when a player should have been able to return the ball across the net but fails to do so because of his or her own mistake.

Venus won just two minor tournaments in 2004. A year later, at Wimbledon 2005, Venus won a hard-fought title, outdueling Lindsay Davenport during a match that spanned nearly three hours. At one point, Venus faced match point, meaning that if she failed to return Davenport's serve she would have lost the tournament. But she stroked the serve back to her opponent with a powerful backhand. Her gutsy play seemed to sap the life out of Davenport's game; a half hour later, Davenport swatted one of Venus's shots into the net, and the match was over. It was Venus's first Grand Slam victory since the 2001 U.S. Open. Her victory in England boosted her ranking to eighth in the world; before Wimbledon, her ranking had fallen to sixteenth. Said Davenport,

> **"Every time the chips were down for Venus, she played unbelievably. I thought I played really well. I thought I had a lot of chances, and I felt like she never allowed me to take advantage of those chances. "**

The year did not go as well for Serena. In January 2005, she made something of a comeback by beating Davenport to win the Australian Open, but then ankle and knee ailments continued to plague her throughout the year and she entered few tournaments.

## ➤ REALITY SHOW STARS ❮

Following Wimbledon, the sisters' lives were very much in the public eye thanks to their agreement to appear in a reality show on the ABC Family network. The show, *Venus & Serena: For Real,* ran weekly during the summer of 2005. Fans got to follow the sisters as they practiced on the court and spent time at home or, in Venus's case, at the office of her design company.

In one humorous episode, Serena caught her dog eating her dinner. In another episode, she broke up with her boyfriend, film director Brett Ratner, on camera. Serena said the sisters agreed to appear in the series because they wanted to show their

An exuberant Venus Williams shows her delight as she displays her trophy at the 2005 Wimbledon tournament. She had battled her way to reach the women's singles final of the Grand Slam event, ultimately facing Lindsay Davenport, then world ranked at number one, on July 2. Williams beat her opponent, 4-6, 7-6, 9-7.

young female fans that women could be successful and independent. She said:

> ❝We consider ourselves role models and we always thought that a lot of teenagers and a lot of

pre-teens look up to us and say, 'I want to be just like them. They're positive and they're fun.' And yet, we know how to split the competitive side and the fun side. So we thought that would be a good aspect to a show for a lot of teen girls out there. **"**

Serena poses with her boyfriend, film director Brett Ratner, in 2004. The two began dating that year but officially split a year later. At that time Ratner was best known as the director of the comedies *Family Man* (2000), *Rush Hour 2* (2001) and *After the Sunset* (2004). He later directed *X-Men: The Last Stand* (2006) and *Rush Hour 3* (2007).

Venus and Serena also reached out to their young fans by writing two books. In 2004, they produced their first collaboration, *How to Play Tennis*, which served as an instruction manual for young players. They gave tips on how to hold the racket, how to hit a lob, and how to stroke a smash shot. A year later, the sisters wrote *Serving from the Hip*, which is a book of advice for teenage girls on how to aim high and succeed. In the book, the sisters provided tips for readers on how to look after their own money, how to build confidence and self-respect, how to maintain personal hygiene, and how to pick their friends. They also stressed the importance of staying in school. Said Venus:

**CROSS-CURRENTS**

To learn more about some other brothers and sisters who have succeeded at the same sport, read "Siblings in Sports." Go to page 54. ▶▶

> **It's one of the most important things that we've done in our lives. It was something that we had to do to pass on our knowledge, what we've gone through.**

*Serving from the Hip* also provided some dating tips to teen girls—a subject Venus and Serena knew something about because, despite their hectic schedules, each sister did find time for a social life. When it came to boyfriends, both sisters tried to guard their privacy carefully. Nevertheless, their names would surface in the **tabloid** press from time to time. Since her relationship with Brett Ratner ended, Serena has been rumored to be in a relationship with actor Jackie Long, whose latest film credits include roles in *Soul Men*, *Love for Sale*, *Doorman*, and *Who's Deal?* Other celebrities who have been linked romantically to Serena include football player LeVar Arrington, ESPN football commentator Keyshawn Johnson, NBA star Corey Maggette, and Major League pitcher C. C. Sabathia.

As for Venus, her relationships have been featured far less in the tabloids. Her longtime boyfriend is professional golfer Hank Kuehne. Kuehne said:

> **Love would be a fair way to describe our relationship. She is one of the most sincere, wonderful and caring women I have ever met and I enjoy every moment with her.**

**Venus and her boyfriend, golfer Hank Kuehne, arrive at Wimbledon in June 2007. He has said of Venus, "There's no one [who] works harder, on or off the court. She's going to be around for a while and play at the top level for as long as she wants to."**

## ≫ A SUCCESSFUL COMEBACK ≪

Their professional and social lives may have been busy and glamorous, but back on the court the sisters continued to struggle to return to top form. For Venus and Serena, 2006 turned out to be mostly a washout. Due to injuries that continued to nag the two stars, as well as their off-the-court commitments, neither sister played in many tournaments. In fact, following her 2005 win in the Australian Open, Serena did not win another tournament until early 2007, when she again won the competition in Melbourne. This time she defeated young Russian sensation Maria Sharapova, who was the second-ranked player in the world. Serena had entered the tournament in 81st place in the world tennis rankings.

In her match against Sharapova, Serena found the quickness and power returning to her game. Clearly, she had recovered from her injuries and could perform at 100 percent. Before the match, tennis insiders wondered whether Serena's career was nearing an end. Her decisive win over Sharapova put those rumors to rest. Said Serena:

> **❝I love doubters. I have a lot of people even close to me who doubt. I love doubters. More than anything what I love, besides obviously winning, is proving people wrong.❞**

In making her successful comeback, Serena had simply gotten serious about tennis again. Since 2002 and 2003, tennis insiders had been wondering when she would regain her championship-caliber play. Indeed, one of the major names in tennis, 1970s champion Chris Evert, openly questioned Serena's dedication to the game, arguing that somebody with Serena's athleticism and talent was too important to tennis to be spending time doing other things. In a letter to Serena published in a 2006 issue of *Tennis* magazine, Evert wrote:

> **❝I don't see how acting and designing clothes can compare with the pride of being the best tennis player in the world. Your other accomplishments just can't measure up to what you can do with a racket in your hand.❞**

## ⪼ FOURTH WIN AT WIMBLEDON ⪻

Venus also hit a dry spell in 2006. Her next tournament win wasn't until Wimbledon in 2007, where she defeated young French tennis star Marion Bartoli in straight sets. Like her sister, Venus's triumph at Wimbledon marked a return to the power game she had developed during her peak years. Many of her serves to Bartoli were clocked at more than 120 miles (193 kilometers) per hour. In

**On July 5, 2008, Venus played her sister Serena in yet another Grand Slam final match. In the end, Venus prevailed, winning her fifth women's singles Wimbledon championship, 7-5, 6-4. At the time, she said of Serena: "I'll help her with anything. I just won't give her tips on how to beat me."**

comparison, Major League baseball's hardest throwing fastball pitchers usually hurl the ball at around 100 miles (161 km) per hour. After the match, Bartoli admitted to being overwhelmed by Venus's serves. She said:

❝Venus played some unbelievable tennis. She reached some balls like I've never seen one person reach, and she would hit it harder back to me. She served 120 miles per hour on the first serve, sometimes hurting my wrist so badly because the ball was coming so fast to me. So I really tried my best, but it's not possible to beat her.❞

After playing against each other in the women's singles final of the 2008 Wimbledon championship, Venus and Serena joined forces to compete in the women's doubles final. The two sisters soon defeated Lisa Raymond of the United States and Samantha Stosur of Australia, 6-2, 6-2. The victory was their third women's doubles title at Wimbledon.

Venus's victory at Wimbledon marked the fourth time she had won that Grand Slam event. Counting Serena's two victories at Wimbledon in 2002 and 2003, only twice from 2000 to 2007 had a player other than Venus or Serena won at Wimbledon.

Their comebacks signaled that the Williams sisters were once again forces to be reckoned with in the tennis world. By early 2008, Venus was ranked seventh in the world, while Serena held the ninth position in the rankings.

## ⟫ MANY YEARS AHEAD ⟪

Clearly, both sisters have recommitted themselves to tennis. In 2008, they started playing as doubles partners again, which they had done only sporadically since 2003. At one time, Venus and Serena were the teen sensations of tennis. Now, both are a bit older, and they find themselves playing against such young stars as Serbians Jelena Jankovic and Ana Ivanovic and Russians Maria Sharapova and Svetlana Kuznetsova. Like the Williams sisters, these young players use their athleticism and strength to blast their shots past their opponents. It seems that Venus and Serena can no longer lay claim to the hardest serves in women's tennis.

Still, Venus and Serena are looking forward to playing against the new competition. Both stars have said they hope to play into their thirties. Venus said:

> **❝I'm not going away. I'm not retiring before 33. I've thought about it already. I'm not giving up my great job. I like it. I'm fortunate. I'm blessed, and I love being out there. ❞**

# The Tragedy of Marion Jones

Venus and Serena Williams weren't the only American athletes to win accolades at the 2000 Olympics. While the sisters made short work of their opponents on the tennis court, track-and-field star Marion Jones proved to be a dominating force in her Olympic events.

Marion Jones was born on October 12, 1975, in Los Angeles, California. From a young age, she was an outstanding athlete. In high school and college, she starred both on the basketball court and in track-and-field events. Marion emerged as an international track star when she won the 100-meter sprint at the 1997 World Championships.

Before the 2000 Olympics, Marion predicted that she would win five gold medals. Although she did not accomplish this feat, she did finish with three gold medals and two bronze medals in sprinting and long jumping. She became the first female track-and-field athlete to win five medals at the Olympics.

Unfortunately, a dark cloud would soon gather over Marion's accomplishments. After the games ended, news reports surfaced suggesting that she had used steroids to prepare for the Olympics. Steroids are drugs that help build up muscle mass, and athletes who use steroids can often run faster, lift heavier weights, hit baseballs farther, and generally improve their performances. Virtually all professional, college, and amateur sports leagues have banned the use of steroids and similar performance-enhancing drugs. The effects can be dangerous, and their use in competitions is considered unfair.

When federal investigators started looking into the allegations, Jones denied taking the drugs or obtaining them from the Bay Area Laboratory Cooperative, or BALCO. This California company was suspected of providing steroids to a number of athletes, including baseball player Barry Bonds. Later, the government investigation revealed that Marion had taken the drugs and lied to investigators. She was charged with perjury, or having given false information to police.

Marion pleaded guilty to the charge in 2007, and tearfully apologized to her fans and teammates for letting them down. A short time later, she was sentenced to six months in prison. She was also forced to relinquish the medals she won in Sydney as well as all the other medals and awards she won in subsequent competitions. The International Olympic Committee also banned her from competing in future Olympic events.

(Go back to page 9.) ◀◀

# The Grand Slam

Dozens of professional tennis tournaments are held each year, but four stand out from the others and are known as the "Grand Slams." These are the U.S. Open in Flushing Meadows, New York, the French Open in Paris, the Australian Open in Melbourne, and Wimbledon in Great Britain.

The four Grand Slam tournaments carry the most prestige and tradition. Their prizes are also larger than those offered in other tournaments, and they count for more in the international rankings for tennis players. After winning the mixed doubles title at Wimbledon in 1998, Serena Williams jumped from being the 100th-ranked female player in the world to the 21st-ranked player.

Only three women have won all four Grand Slam titles in a single year: Maureen Connelly in 1953, Margaret Smith Court in 1970, and Steffi Graf in 1988. Serena Williams won all four titles in a row but not in the same year. She scored victories in the French Open, Wimbledon, and U.S. Open in 2002 and the Australian Open in January 2003. She is still regarded as a Grand Slam winner, though. In fact, her four victories over two years are known as the "Serena Slam."

(Go back to page 14.)

*A 2007 view of Arthur Ashe Stadium, located in Flushing Meadows, New York City, at the Billie Jean King National Tennis Center. The center is home to the last Grand Slam event of the tennis season—the U.S. Open. Each year in August and September the world's top players, vying for the coveted championship title, compete at the event.*

## The Bump

When Venus Williams advanced to the finals of the U.S. Open in 1997 as an unseeded player, her spectacular accomplishment was overshadowed by an ugly, off-court spat with Romanian tennis star Irina Spirlea.

As the tournament proceeded, Venus found herself uncomfortable around the other players, who regarded the unseeded youngster as something of an upstart. There were some icy moments in the women's locker room between Venus and other players, particularly Spirlea.

Then, during their semifinal match as the two players were changing sides between games, Venus and Spirlea bumped into one another. Over the years, there has been much speculation about the bump—whether it was accidental or whether one player meant to intimidate the other. Venus has shouldered much of the blame, as many believe the bump was actually a shove by Venus.

Yet she has always insisted the bump was inadvertent—at least on her part. Venus felt that the incident gave her an unfair reputation. She says that she and her sister are not about intimidation tactics on the court. They are about having fun.

(Go back to page 14.)

## Wimbledon

Football has the Super Bowl, baseball has the World Series, and hockey has the Stanley Cup. Wimbledon is only one of the four Grand Slam tennis tournaments, but it is the most prestigious tournament of the year, and it is the competition that truly defines the sport.

It is the oldest competition in professional tennis, dating back to 1877 when the All England Croquet and Lawn Tennis Club, now familiarly known as the All England Club, sponsored its first tournament at club headquarters in Wimbledon, England, near London. At the time, only men were permitted to play.

The first Wimbledon title was won by Spencer Gore. Two hundred spectators attended the tournament. Less than a decade later, women were allowed in the competition. In 1884, Maud Wilson won the first women's title.

Since then, Wimbledon has been the scene of some of the fiercest competition in the tennis world. Among the rivalries featured in the finals on Wimbledon's "Centre Court" were matches involving Arthur Ashe and Jimmy Connors in 1975, Martina Navratilova and Chris Evert in 1978, Bjorn Borg and John McEnroe in 1980, and Roger Federer and Pete Sampras in 2001.

(Go back to page 20.)

## Trailblazers

Compared to sports like basketball, baseball, football, and track and field, tennis historically featured few African-American stars. Today, thanks to the efforts of early pioneers in the sport, professional tennis is not as limited as it was in the past.

The first important African-American tennis star was Althea Gibson (1927–2003), who in August 1950 became the first black woman to compete on the world tennis tour. During the 1950s, Althea won five Grand Slam events and was the top-ranked female player in the world in 1957. When she won at Wimbledon in 1957, becoming the first African American to win the event, the *New York Times* wrote in an editorial:

**"It would be even more to the credit of all of us if there were no occasion to mention her race. But there has to be a first time when barriers are broken down, and when this happens it is news in itself and the time for congratulation."**

*Despite the racial barriers that existed during the 1950s, Althea Gibson pursued a career as a professional tennis player. She was the first African American to play in Grand Slam events, competing in the U.S. Championships in 1950 and at Wimbledon in 1951. In the course of her career she won 11 Grand Slam titles.*

After Gibson retired from the sport in 1958, the next major African-American tennis star to appear was Arthur Ashe (1943–1993). Arthur's 1968 victory in the U.S. Open made him the first black man to win a Grand Slam singles title. He would go on to win two other

Grand Slam events as well as many other tournaments during the 1970s. Arthur also became involved in the civil rights movement, and was well known for his work to help others. After his early death at the age of 50, the stadium in Flushing Meadows where the U.S. Open is played was named in his memory.

The trails blazed by Gibson and Ashe have enabled other African-American athletes to break into international tennis competition. During the 1980s and 1990s, Zina Garrison rose to as high as fourth in world rankings; she won several tournaments and, in 1990, advanced to the Wimbledon finals. On her way to the finals, she defeated Monica Seles and Steffi Graf but lost to Martina Navratilova.

In contemporary play, some of the African-American players who have joined Venus and Serena on the women's circuit are Chandra Rubin, Alexandra Stevenson, Brittany Augustine, Angela Haynes, Jamea Jackson, Raquel Kops-Jones, Asia Muhammad, Shenay Perry, Jewel Peterson, Ahsha Rolle, and Mashona Washington. Among the rising black stars in men's play are James Blake, Marcus Fugate, Levar Harper-Griffith, Scoville Jenkins, Lesley Joseph, Timothy Neilly, Phillip Simmonds, Mashiska Washington, and Donald Young.

(Go back to page 23.)

# Jehovah's Witnesses

Venus and Serena Williams are Jehovah's Witnesses, members of a religious sect established more than a century ago. The denomination takes its name from early Christian translations of the Hebrew name for God. It is based on the teachings of Charles Taze Russell, a Protestant minister who lived in Pittsburgh during the late 19th century and early 20th century. Although Jehovah's Witnesses are sometimes identified as Christians, they do not share some of the core beliefs of mainstream Christian churches.

There are believed to be nearly 7 million members of the Jehovah's Witness church in more than 200 countries. Other Jehovah's Witnesses of note include pop singers Michael Jackson, Janet Jackson, Prince, Geri Hallowell, and Selena; model Naomi Campbell; and film stars Damon, Shawn, Marlon and Keenan Ivory Wayans. Also, President Dwight D. Eisenhower was a member of the faith when he was a child.

Jehovah's Witnesses are expected to proselytize, or actively help spread the faith to others. To carry out their duty to proselytize, most members of the church knock on doors or pass out church literature in public places. Venus and Serena make phone calls. They tried knocking on doors, but too many people wanted their autographs.

(Go back to page 30.)

# Favorite Hobbies

Away from court, Venus Williams loves to surf, play the guitar, sew, and cook, when she is not tending to her interior design business. Her culinary specialties are meat dishes, vegetarian meals, and desserts. Says her sister Serena:

> **"One of my personal favorites, along with her delectable braised pork chops, would have to be her vegetarian tofu burritos. But I can't forget to mention her flawless Jello."**

As for Serena, when she has spare time she likes to read—she has read all the *Harry Potter* books, although her favorite author is Maya Angelou. She also likes to watch movies and football. Mostly, though, she likes to shop and admits to a "mild shopping addiction." Says Venus:

> **"When I walk into her closet, I begin to wonder whether the 'mild shopping addiction' has turned into a serious problem. Everywhere I turn there are new purses, unworn stiletto and Gucci and Sergio Rossi shoes, rows of leather pants (all in different cuts), taffeta gowns, silver chain belts, and even a few of my things that I'm sure won't be returned."**

(Go back to page 33.) ◀◀

# Siblings in Sports

Venus and Serena Williams are among a long list of siblings who have excelled in sports. The list of famous siblings who have faced each other from time to time probably starts back in the 1940s, when Joe DiMaggio, an All-Star outfielder for the New York Yankees, occasionally found himself taking the field against his brother Dominic, who played for the Boston Red Sox. A third brother, Vince, also had a Major League career.

In more recent years, brothers Peyton and Eli Manning have occasionally faced one another on the football field. Both are quarterbacks. In 2007, Peyton Manning led the Indianapolis Colts to a Super Bowl victory; a year later, his brother quarterbacked the New York Giants to victory in football's biggest game. Before his retirement following the 2007 season, New York Giants running back Tiki Barber often dodged the tackles of his twin brother, Ronde, a defensive back for the Tampa Bay Buccaneers.

Other siblings who have competed in sports include twin Olympic gymnasts Paul and Morgan Hamm; men's tennis stars Bob and Mike Bryan, who are also twins; and Major League catchers Jose, Benjie, and Yadier Molina. Former basketball player Reggie Miller was a star of the NBA, while his sister, Cheryl Miller, starred in women's basketball in college and coached on the professional level in the Women's NBA. (Go back to page 43.) ◀◀

# Equal Rights on the Court

Venus and Serena Williams have each earned more than $18 million in prize money during their tennis careers. However, there is no question that if they had been male players they could have earned more—perhaps much more.

Even though women's tennis is a major international sport, for many years the sponsors of major tournaments reserved the biggest purses for the male players. In 1968, the first year in which Wimbledon offered cash prizes to players, men's champion Rod Laver took home a purse of $4,000 while Billie Jean King, the winner of the women's competition, was awarded just $1,500.

Over the years, the size of the purses has increased dramatically. By 2008, for example, the total prize money awarded to all players at Wimbledon was more than $22 million. Meanwhile, other tournaments that had been offering better purses to male players slowly dropped that practice and made sure players of both genders were paid equal sums. Still, as recently as 2006, Wimbledon and the French Open continued to pay smaller purses to female players. In 2006, the men's winner, Roger Federer, earned $1.17 million at Wimbledon, while the purse paid to the women's winner, Amelie Mauresmo, was about $70,000 less.

As the 2006 competition at Wimbledon approached, Venus pressed the promoters to guarantee equal purses to both genders. In a letter published in the *Times* of London shortly before the tournament, she wrote that she had always told young girls that their talents were equal to those of men. Said Venus:

> **"My fear is that Wimbledon is loudly and clearly sending the opposite message: 128 men and 128 women compete in the singles main draw at Wimbledon; the All England Club is saying that the accomplishments of the 128 women are worth less than those of the 128 men. It diminishes the stature and credibility of such a great event in the eyes of all women."**

The letter in the *Times* caught the notice of British Prime Minister Tony Blair, who agreed to support Venus in the campaign to win equal purses for women. Under pressure from Blair and other British political leaders, Wimbledon officials agreed to change the tournament's policy. Starting in 2007, Wimbledon would equalize the purses for male and female athletes. At the same time, French officials ended gender discrimination at the French Open as well.

(Go back to page 45.)

**1980**  Venus Williams is born June 17 in Lynwood, California.

**1981**  Serena Williams is born September 26 in Saginaw, Michigan.

**1991**  After teaching tennis to his daughters, Richard Williams moves the family to Florida so Venus and Serena can receive professional coaching.

**1994**  Venus plays in her first professional tournament.

**1995**  Serena turns professional.

**1996**  While playing hooky from school, Serena falls off her skateboard and injures a wrist; the injury forces her to compensate by developing a much quicker game on the court.

**1997**  Entering the U.S. Open as an unseeded player, Venus makes it to the finals but loses on September 7 to Martina Hingis.

**1998**  Serena and Max Mirnyi win the mixed-doubles title at Wimbledon on July 5; at 16, Serena is the youngest doubles winner in the history of the tournament.

**1999**  Serena wins the sisters' first Grand Slam singles competition on September 11, defeating Martina Hingis at the U.S. Open.

**2000**  Playing in doubles competition on September 21 at the Olympic Games in Sydney, Australia, Venus and Serena win the gold medal; Venus also wins the gold in singles competition.

**2001**  After winning tournaments on July 6 at Wimbledon and September 8 at the U.S. Open, Venus is the top-ranked women's tennis player in the world.

**2002**  Serena defeats Venus in the finals of the French Open on June 8; the victory marks the first of four straight Grand Slam titles that Serena will win, which propels her into the top ranking in women's tennis for 57 weeks.

**2003**  Yetunde Price, Venus and Serena's older half sister, dies from a gunshot wound on September 13; after two trials that end in hung juries, the killer pleads guilty to manslaughter and is sentenced to 15 years in prison.

**2004**  Hobbled most of the year by injuries, Venus concentrates on her interior design business while Serena opens a fashion studio and also accepts acting roles.

**2005**  Serena stages a comeback by winning the Australian Open on January 29; Venus also returns to the top rankings by defeating Lindsay Davenport at Wimbledon on July 2.

**2007**  After a year of injuries and pursuits off the court in which tennis insiders doubt Serena's commitment to the game, Serena wins the Australian Open on January 27; Venus wins Wimbledon on July 7.

**2008**  News media reports suggest Venus and professional golfer Hank Kuehne plan to wed.

## Grand Slam Singles Titles

**Serena Williams**

**1999** U.S. Open

**2002** French Open
Wimbledon
U.S. Open

**2003** Australian Open
Wimbledon

**2005** Australian Open

**2007** Australian Open

**Venus Williams**

**2000** Wimbledon
U.S. Open

**2001** Wimbledon
U.S. Open

**2005** Wimbledon

**2007** Wimbledon

**2008** Wimbledon

## Grand Slam Doubles Titles

**Shared by Serena and Venus Williams**

**1999** French Open
U.S. Open

**2000** Wimbledon

**2001** Australian Open

**2002** Wimbledon

**2003** Australian Open

**2008** Wimbledon

## Grand Slam Mixed Doubles Titles

**Serena Williams**

**1998** Wimbledon, with Max Mirnyi
U.S. Open, with Max Mirnyi

**Venus Williams**

**1998** Australian Open, with Justin Gimelstob
French Open, with Justin Gimelstob

# ACCOMPLISHMENTS & AWARDS

## Awards

### Venus Williams

**1997**   Women's Tennis Association Newcomer of the Year

**2000**   Women's Tennis Association Player of the Year
With Serena, Women's Tennis Association Doubles Team of the Year
*Sports Illustrated* Sportswoman of the Year

**2001**   ESPN Espy for Best Female Tennis Player

**2002**   ESPN Espy for Best Female Tennis Player

**2006**   ESPN Espy for Best Female Tennis Player
Black Entertainment Television Female Athlete of the Year

### Serena Williams

**1998**   Women's Tennis Association Newcomer of the Year

**1999**   Women's Tennis Association Most Improved Player

**2000**   With Venus, Women's Tennis Association Doubles Team of the Year

**2002**   Women's Tennis Association Player of the Year
International Tennis Federation World Champion
Associated Press Female Athlete of the Year

**2003**   Laureus Academy of Monto Carlo Sportswoman of the Year
ESPN Espy for Best Female Tennis Player

**2004**   ESPN Espy for Best Female Tennis Player
Women's Tennis Association Comeback Player of the Year

**2007**   Black Entertainment Television Female Athlete of the Year

Corbett, Sara. "It's Not Easy Being Displaced as No. 1, Especially When It's by Your Little Sister." *New York Times Magazine* (Jan. 12, 2003): p. 27.

Dominus, Susan. "Dangerous When Interested." *New York Times Play Magazine* (Aug. 19, 2007): p. 48.

Edmondson, Jacqueline. *Venus and Serena Williams: A Biography*. Westport, CT: Greenwood Press, 2005.

Harris, Cecil, and Larryette Kyle-DeBose. *Charging the Net: A History of Blacks in Tennis from Althea Gibson and Arthur Ashe to the Williams Sisters*. Chicago: Ivan R. Dee, 2007.

Peyser, Marc, and Allison Samuels. "Venus and Serena Against the World." *Newsweek* vol. 132, no. 8 (Aug. 24, 1998): p. 44.

Schoenfeld, Bruce. "The Venus Trap." *Tennis* vol. 39, no. 6 (July 2003): p. 40.

Williams, Venus, and Serena Williams. *How to Play Tennis*. New York: DK Children, 2004.

Williams, Venus, and Serena Williams and Hilary Beard. *Serving from the Hip: 10 Rules for Living, Loving, and Winning*. Boston: Houghton Mifflin, 2005.

## Web Sites

### http://www.williamssisters.org

The official Web site for Venus and Serena Williams offers visitors biographies of the sisters, photos of the two tennis stars, and results of some of their recent matches.

### http://www.sonyericssonwtatour.com/1/

Sponsored by Sony Ericsson Corp., the Women's Tennis Association maintains this Web site where visitors can find results of recent tournaments, a schedule of events, and the current rankings of the best women tennis players in the world.

### http://www.vstarrinteriors.com

This Web site is for V Starr Interiors, the interior design company owned by Venus Williams. By following the link for portfolio, visitors can see photos of some of the tennis star's design projects.

### http://www.aneresdesigns.com/

At the Web site for Aneres Designs, the fashion design company founded by Serena Williams, visitors can see some of the clothes Serena has designed. Models featured on the site include Serena as well as singers Brandy and Kelly Rowland from Destiny's Child.

### http://www.wimbledon.org/en_GB/index.html

At the Web site maintained by the All England Club, visitors can find a history of the Wimbledon tournament, news about the annual tournament, and videos of recent matches.

**abdominal**—relating to the midsection of the human body.

**asphalt**—substance composed of oil, gravel, and other materials that is used to pave the surfaces of streets, parking lots, basketball courts, playgrounds, and tennis courts.

**backhand**—in tennis, a stroke made by a player who must reach across his or her body to return a ball; many players hit their backhands two-handed, swinging their rackets more or less like baseball bats.

**bodyguard**—an individual hired to provide protection against harm or kidnapping.

**crack cocaine**—an inexpensive form of cocaine that is manufactured in crystal form, usually ingested by smoking in a pipe.

**endorsement**—an agreement by a celebrity, athlete, or other noted person to back a private company's product or service, usually by appearing in TV commercials and other advertisements on behalf of the product.

**forehand**—in tennis, a stroke made from the same side of the body as the hand holding the racket.

**gold medal**—top award in Olympic competition; other awards are the silver medal for second place and bronze for third.

**journalists**—professionals who report and write news for newspapers, magazines, radio and TV broadcasts, and Internet outlets.

**manslaughter**—the killing of a human being without intent.

**match point**—the last point needed in tennis in order for one side to win a match.

**mixed doubles**—a tennis partners team consisting of a man and a woman.

**Olympic Games**—an international athletic competition staged every four years; athletes compete as teams representing their countries.

**straight sets**—two tennis sets won consecutively, meaning the match was won without the victor ever having lost a set.

**suburb**—a populated area located just outside a major city; residents of the suburb usually maintain social or economic ties to the city.

**tabloid**—style of journalism that concentrates on scandal, celebrity news, and sensational crime.

**tournament**—tennis competition in which players compete in singles and doubles play; usually, it is decided through a series of elimination rounds until just two players or teams remain for the final match.

**trauma**—an injury, or a state of mental distress.

**volley**—in tennis, a ball that is hit back by a player before it bounces.

**page 6** "I couldn't type, I couldn't . . ." S. L. Price, "Simply Super," *Sports Illustrated for Women*, 2 no. 5 (November/December 2000), p. 84.

**page 8** "If you're playing a college . . ." Juan C. Rodriguez, "Battle of the Sexes II?" *Miami Herald* (August 31, 2000), p. 8-D.

**page 9** "We worked so hard . . ." Bud Collins, "Sisters Keep Gold in Family," *Boston Globe* (September 29, 2000), p. E-3.

**page 13** "You could see they were . . ." Cecil Harris and Larryette Kyle-DeBose, *Charging the Net: A History of Blacks in Tennis from Althea Gibson to the Williams Sisters* (Chicago: Ivan R. Dee, 2007), p. 22.

**page 16** "I guess I was nervous . . ." Greg Garber, "It's Hingis in Another Grand Finish," *Hartford Courant* (September 8, 1997), p. C-1.

**page 16** "I was thinking . . ." Jeff Williams, "Quotes: The Second Sister Isn't Playing Second," *Newsday* (September 12, 1999), p. C-3.

**page 17** "I just took on a new . . ." S. L. Price, "Simply Super," p. 84.

**page 20** "I never would allow that . . ." "A Perfect Match," *CNN.com* (2004). http://www.cnn.com/CNN/Programs/people/shows/williams/profile.html

**page 20** "She takes losing harder . . ." Bud Collins, "Victory Is Bittersweet, But She'll Take It," *Boston Globe* (July 7, 2000), p. E-1.

**page 22** "It's really great because . . ." Steve Wilstein, "Venus Wins in Straight Sets; Defeats Davenport to Become First Black Women's Wimbledon Champion in 42 Years." *Pittsburgh Post-Gazette* (July 9, 2000), p. D-1.

**page 23** "It's never been easy for me . . ." Bruce Schoenfeld, "The Venus Trap." *Tennis* 39, no. 6 (July 2003), p. 40.

**page 24** "I don't really pay . . ." Dennis Passa, "Accused Williams Stalker Arrested at Wimbledon," *USA Today* (July 4, 2002). http://www.usatoday.com/sports/tennis/02wim/2002-07-04-stromeyer.htm#more

**page 25** "Would [anything] stop me . . ." "Serena Stalker Deported" *CBS News* (September 6, 2002). http://www.cbsnews.com/stories/2002/09/06/entertainment/main521152.shtml

**page 26** "It's been sloppy . . ." "A Perfect Match," *CNN.com*.

**page 26** "Venus is more than a great . . ." Serena Williams, "She's Got It!" *Tennis* 36, no. 10 (December 2000/January 2001), p. 24.

**page 27** "Tennis is just a game . . ." Stephen Borelli, "It's Venus, Serena at Love," *USA Today* (September 9, 2001).

**page 27** "So many minorities think . . ." Marc Peyser and Allison Samuels, "Venus and Serena Against the World," *Newsweek* 132, no. 8 (August 24, 1998), p. 44.

**page 29** "I wanted to get away . . ." Sara Corbett, "It's Not Easy Being Displaced as No. 1, Especially When It's by Your Little Sister" *New York Times Magazine* (January 12, 2003), p. 27.

**page 33** "I love tennis. It's always . . ." Christopher Clarey, "Williamses Test a Life Without Any Games," *New York Times* (August 28, 2003), p. D-1.

**page 34** "When [Venus and Serena] received . . ." Bill Hewitt, Frank Swertlow, Lyndon Stambler, Vicki Sheff-Cahan, and Lori Rozsa, "Fatal Volley" *People* 60, no. 13, (September 29, 2003), p. 63.

**page 35** "No one knows that pain . . ." Liz Robbins, "Serena Williams Decides It's Time to Take Hold of Her Life," *Toronto Star* (August 27, 2006), p. B-12.

**page 37** "It's not just the [sisters'] . . ." "A Perfect Match," *CNN.com*.

**page 40** "Every time the chips . . ." Christopher Clarey, "In an Epic Wimbledon Final, Williams Prevails," *New York Times* (July 3, 2005), p. 1.

**page 41** "We consider ourselves role models . . ." Miki Turner, "Venus and Serena Keep It Real" *ESPN.com* (July 19, 2005). http://sports.espn.go.com/espn/page3/story?page=turner/williams/050719

**page 43** "It's one of the most important . . ." Yanick Rice Lamb, "Sister Act" *Black Issues Book Review* 7, no. 5 (September/October 2005), p. 22.

**page 43** "Love would be a fair way . . ." Alex Tresniowski, Amy Elisa Keigh, and Eunice Oh, "Venus Rising" *People* 68, no. 10 (September 3, 2007), p. 115.

**page 45** "I love doubters . . ." William C. Rhoden, "Riding Her Will, Instead of Just Skill," *New York Times* (January 27, 2007), p. D-1.

**page 45** "I don't see how acting . . ." Susan Dominus, "Dangerous When Interested," *New York Times Play Magazine* (August 19, 2007), p. 48.

**page 47** "Venus played some unbelievable tennis . . ." Bud Collins, "Venus Best, Brightest—Starry Williams Beats Bartoli to Win Fourth Wimbledon Title," *Boston Globe* (July 8, 2007), p. C-1.

**page 48** "I'm not going away . . ." Clarey, "Williamses Test a Life Without Any Games," D-1.

**page 52** "It would be even more . . ." Harris and Kyle-DeBose, *Charging the Net*, p. 64.

**page 54** "One of my personal favorites . . ." Williams, "She's Got It!" p. 24.

**page 54** "When I walk into her closet . . ." Venus Williams, "The Little Sister That Could" *Tennis* 36, no. 10 (December 2000/January 2001), p. 26.

**page 55** "My fear is that Wimbledon . . ." Venus Williams, "Wimbledon Has Sent Me a Message: I'm Only a Second-Class Champion," *Times* (June 26, 2006). http://www.timesonline.co.uk/tol/sport/tennis/article679416.ece

Numbers in **bold italics** refer to captions.

**Hal Marcovitz** has written more than 100 books for young readers. He lives in Chalfont, Pennsylvania, with his wife, Gail, and daughter, Ashley. He has also written about Derek Jeter in the MODERN ROLE MODELS series.

## PICTURE CREDITS